DATE DUE			

5901.

Planning for a
SUSTAINABLE
FUTURE

Helen Belmont

Smart Apple Media

This book has been published in cooperation with Franklin Watts.

Editor: Jennifer Schofield

Consultant: Steve Watts
(FRGS, Principal Lecturer University of Sunderland)

Art director: Jonathan Hair

Design: Mo Choy

Artwork: John Alston

Picture researcher: Kathy Lockley

Acknowledgements

© Alfred d'Amato/Panos Pictures 40. Art Directors & TRIP Photo Library 13, 38. Ross Barnett/Lonely Planet Images 35.

Sarah Clifford, Piedra Blanca Community EcoTourism Project. www.piedrablanca.org 37. Neil Cooper/Still Pictures 11.

Nigel Dickenson/Still Pictures 41. © Digital Vision COVER, 3, 9, 17, © Natalie Forbes/Corbis 39. Courtesy of the Grameen Foundation 43.

Chris Fairclough 24.Jeff Greenberg/Lonely Planet Images 28. Robert Harding Picture Library 18, 31, 36. © Collart Herve/Corbis Sygma 7.

Daniel Heuclin/NHPA 15. © Ed Quinn/Corbis 34. © Roger Ressmeyer/Corbis 23. © Karen Robinson/Panos Pictures 32. Jorgen Schytte/

Still Pictures 10. Jonathan & Angela Scott/NHPA 8. Sean Sprague/Still Pictures 27. Volker Steger/Science Photo Library 42.

Manfred Vollmer/Still Pictures 19. ©. Phillip Walmuth/Panos Pictures 6.

Published in the United States by Smart Apple Media
2140 Howard Drive West, North Mankato, Minnesota 56003

Library of Congress Cataloging-in-Publication Data

Belmont, Helen.
Planning for a sustainable future / by Helen Belmont.
p. cm. — (Geography skills)
Includes index.
ISBN-13: 978-1-59920-051-4
1. Sustainable development. I. Title.

HC79.E5B445 2007
338.9'27—dc22   2006100028

9 8 7 6 5 4 3 2 1

Contents

Planning for the future

There are approximately six and a half billion people living on the earth. Today, the world population is increasing at the rate of 1.14 percent per year, which means that about 9,000 babies are being born every hour. A growing population puts increasing pressure on limited resources, including food, water, and energy. Since our planet remains the same size, it is important that we plan for the future so that our resources do not run out.

These people are waiting on an overcrowded train platform. How will we get around in the future when there are even more people who want to travel?

People today must be responsible for keeping our planet healthy. These people in Curitiba, Brazil (see page 31) are trading their garbage for bus tickets.

STEWARDSHIP

As individuals, we are all stewards of our planet. This means that we are its guardians, caring for it today and leaving it in good condition for future generations. We can do this by thinking about the way we use the earth's resources, such as oil, metals, water, and wood.

NATIONAL AND INTERNATIONAL STEWARDSHIP

People in government can make laws to protect the environment and to encourage people to become good stewards. This can also be done at an international level.

In 1992, the first international Earth Summit was held in Rio de Janeiro, Brazil. At this meeting, and at others since, representatives from all over the world discussed the condition of the planet. As a response to concerns about damage caused by pollution and the use of too many natural resources, they have agreed on a number of steps that countries could take to help the earth stay healthy.

HELPING HAND
Throughout this book, this helping hand will give you useful tips and hints.

WARNING SIGN
When you see this sign, you should be extra careful when completing the task.

KEY SKILLS
Throughout this book, you will learn different skills. Each skill is represented by one of the following icons:

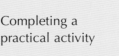 Completing a practical activity

 Analyzing information

Working with graphs, maps, diagrams, and photographs

 Looking at global issues

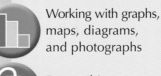 Researching information

 Observing

What is sustainability?

Sustainability is about living in a way that does not damage the earth for future generations. At the Rio de Janeiro Earth Summit and later meetings, politicians discussed how countries around the world are working toward a sustainable future.

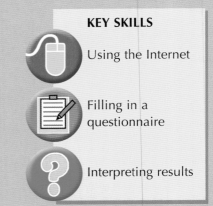

KEY SKILLS

Using the Internet

Filling in a questionnaire

Interpreting results

GETTING THE RIGHT BALANCE

Sustainability can be broken down into three different categories. These categories are based on how people are using the earth's resources with regard to the environment and sustainability. To achieve sustainability, people need to look at all three categories.

The three categories are:
1) Environmental sustainability: protecting the environment—including wildlife and the earth's resources—from pollution and overuse.
2) Social justice: ensuring that people have a good quality of life and maintain it without jeopardizing the earth's resources.
3) Economic well-being: ensuring that people can reach an economically stable quality of life without overusing the earth's resources and endangering the planet.

These giraffes are on the African plains. Protecting natural environments is one of the three categories of sustainability.

ECO FOOTPRINT

We can measure how sustainable our own lives are by calculating the size of our eco footprint. The footprint is the amount of productive land and water needed to sustain one person's lifestyle, including the amount of food they eat, the products that they use and discard, and the amount of energy they use every day. Eco footprints vary tremendously across nations. For example, in the United States, the average eco footprint is 24 global acres (9.9 global ha), while in Mozambique it is 1.2 global acres (0.47 global ha). Today, there is only enough productive area on the earth for us to each have 4.7 global acres (1.9 global ha).

A power station in the U.S. We all use electricity and other sources of power. How much we use is reflected in our eco footprint.

MEASURE YOUR ECO FOOTPRINT

To measure your eco footprint go to www.ecofoot.org. Choose your country and answer the questions. You may need help from a parent, guardian, or teacher. Figure out your eco footprint and then look at what you could do to reduce it. The higher the number, the bigger your negative impact on the earth.

Water: a key resource

Water is essential for life. We use it in many ways: for transportation, in industry and agriculture, to keep our bodies and clothes clean, and to drink. Unfortunately, water is not distributed evenly across the world and many places in less economically developed countries (LEDCs) do not have clean water. So how should we plan for everyone to have clean drinking water in the future?

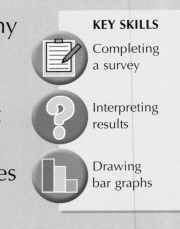

KEY SKILLS

Completing a survey

Interpreting results

Drawing bar graphs

HEALTH EDUCATION

Farmers in some areas of the world need flood water to grow crops, but too much can cause death and destruction. During a flood, drinking water can become polluted with sewage and oil. In some countries, such as Bangladesh, where areas are often flooded, the government and charities are working with local people to teach them about health care. They provide water purification tablets that are used to clean small amounts of water, and they dig special wells to try to reduce the contamination of water.

A water education class in Bangladesh. Children are taught where to collect safe water and what to do after a flood.

DIGGING MORE WELLS

In countries such as Malawi in Africa, there is so little rainfall that many people spend up to three hours a day walking to wells or rivers to collect water for their family. Not only is this extremely hard work, but it also leaves them little time to do anything else. Is this sustainable? Slowly governments and charities are working to dig wells closer to where people live. One charity recently dug 33 wells to supply clean water to 100,000 people in Malawian villages.

Engineers dig a well in Kenya. Wells provide villages with a clean source of water—something that many people take for granted.

WATER QUESTIONNAIRE

Make a survey to learn more about how your friends and family use water. Start by creating a questionnaire similar to the one on the right. Group your answers together and present them with a bar graph. Find out which actions use the least amount of water and encourage people to save water. Repeat the questionnaire at a later date to see how your results have changed.

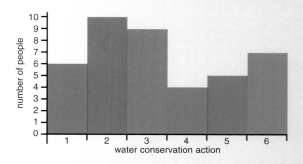

ACTION	YES	NO
1. Do you leave the faucet running while you brush your teeth?		
2. Do you take a shower?		
3. Do you take a bath?		
4. Do you use a hose to clean the car?		
5. Do you use a bucket and sponge to clean the car?		
6. Do you have a full load in the washing machine each time you run it?		

River planning

River systems are part of the water cycle. They transfer rain from drainage basins and eventually carry it to the ocean. People use rivers for hydroelectricity, transporting goods, irrigating crops, and creating reservoirs for drinking water. Geographers are often asked to become involved in making plans for managing rivers.

KEY SKILLS

Writing a report

Looking up global issues

Analyzing information

Using the Internet

INVESTIGATING RIVER USE

Some rivers are enormous and bring vital water to entire countries. Find a map of the Nile River in Egypt to see its size. Use the Internet to find out how important the river is to the people of Egypt. Research the Aswan High Dam and the effect it is having on the Nile River and the surrounding area.

USING THE FLOODPLAIN

The flat land on either side of a river is called the floodplain. When the river floods, mud, or sediment, carried by river water is deposited on the floodplain, making the land fertile, or good for growing crops.

Because the floodplain is flat, it is also good land for building houses and industries.

To use more of the land, farmers and land developers often drain some of the floodplain and alter the course of the river to make it safer and easier to use. In some places, tall banks are built to prevent the river from flooding onto the surrounding land. Dams and barriers also help prevent flooding. However, these changes have unwanted side effects. The wildlife of the rivers can be changed by building, and some types of river plants and animal life may gradually disappear from the area.

Sediment collects behind dams and barriers and does not flow onto floodplains. As a result, the nutrient-rich sediment that the river carries does not fertilize the land.

HOLISTIC PLANNING

While traditional river planning continues in many places, others are now using holistic planning. This planning method looks at the entire river over a full year, not just one part for a few months.

RESEARCH AND REPORT

The Brede River in Denmark is a good example of how a river is holistically managed. The river was straightened to create more farmland. Use the Internet to find out how the Brede River is managed today. Then, write a report on your findings. Your report should include how the river was managed in the past and how it is managed today.

HELPING HAND
Log on to: www.therrc.co.uk/projects/ brede.htm for help researching your report on the Brede River in Denmark.

Farmland and buildings on the floodplain of the Nile River in Egypt. The flooding of the Nile washes fertile sediment onto the land. But because the river is controlled by dams, fewer floods occur and farmers are forced to use more artificial fertilizers.

13

Coastal defense

The sea and the weather constantly erode cliffs, depositing rock material on the beaches below. In time, the rocks break down into smaller fragments, such as pebbles, and eventually into sand. Many places in coastal areas are being protected by different engineering plans that will hopefully preserve the coastline for the future.

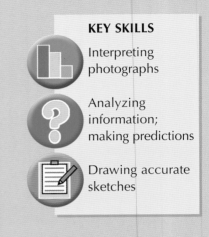

KEY SKILLS

Interpreting photographs

Analyzing information; making predictions

Drawing accurate sketches

HARD ENGINEERING

People who have houses or farmland on the coast want to protect the coastline from erosion. If nothing is done, eventually the land will be washed into the sea. Seawalls, groins, rocks, and other examples of hard engineering solutions are constructed to reduce erosion in one place, but often, these cause problems in other places along the coast. If the coastline in some areas is protected, less sand is produced by erosion. This means that beaches are narrower farther along the coast. Narrower beaches cannot stop waves as effectively, so erosion speeds up where the coastal defenses stop.

BEACH SKETCH

Look at the picture of the groins below. Find out what effects groins have on the coast. Make a drawing of a beach that is being eroded, such as Pensacola Beach, Florida. How would you slow erosion? Look at the examples of soft engineering on the next page. Would you use this solution instead?

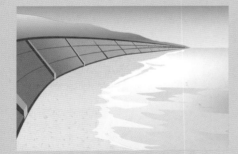

Seawalls
Seawalls are usually made of concrete. They are expensive to build and only prevent erosion of the land behind them, as far as they extend. Eventually, they will also erode.

Groins
Groins are usually made from wood and extend out toward the sea. They help beaches build up, which prevents waves from eroding the coastline. Groins can be expensive to maintain.

Rocks
Boulders or blocks of concrete are used to reduce the impact of waves and slow down land erosion. It can be difficult to obtain rocks and get them into position.

The roots of mangrove trees help hold together the soil and prevent it from being washed away by waves.

SOFT ENGINEERING

Most people agree that hard engineering is not a sustainable solution. Coastlines need to be protected using other methods, such as soft engineering. One method is to allow the coastline to change without building sea defenses or to remove existing sea defenses in some places and restrict building development close to the coast. This soft engineering policy is called "strategic retreat."

It encourages people to move away from the threatened coastal areas by imposing strict planning rules.

Another example of soft engineering is to help nature provide natural sea defenses. For instance, in some areas of Thailand, the Philippines, and on the northern coast of Australia, mangrove forests have been cut down to create beaches for the tourist industry. The mangrove trees

absorb 80 percent of the energy from storm waves, so when they are cut down, the coastal areas are at a much greater risk of erosion and flooding. Today, mangrove forests are being replanted along some coasts and companies are encouraged to stop cutting down trees. The mangrove forests are sustainable solutions because the trees will protect the coastline naturally, without causing any adverse effects.

Forests of the future

Forests are vital to the health of the earth and its people. Trees cover a fifth of all land on the earth and help regulate the gases in the atmosphere by absorbing carbon dioxide and producing oxygen. The roots of trees help prevent the soil from being washed away, and dead, rotting leaves and branches make the soil fertile, so plants can grow. Forests provide a rich habitat for all types of wildlife.

TYPES OF FORESTS

There are many different types of forests around the world. Use the Internet and reference books to find out more about each forest shown on this map. Find out the type of climate each forest has and what the trees look like—for example, trees in rain forests often have tall trunks, large buttress roots, and a canopy of leaves.

This map shows the current location of the world's major forests.

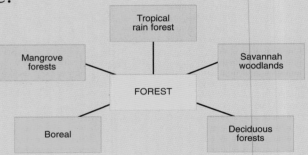

You can display your information on a web diagram, similar to the one above.

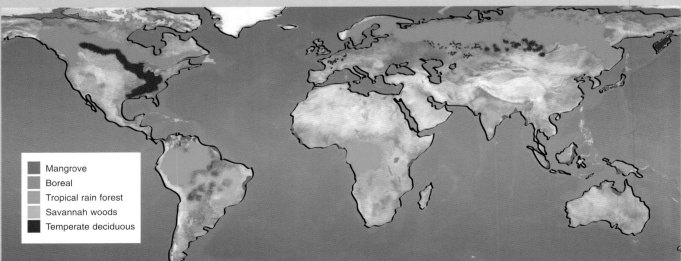

Mangrove
Boreal
Tropical rain forest
Savannah woods
Temperate deciduous

Logging is one of the main contributors to global deforestation.

HELPING HAND
Look at the archive report at:
http://archive.greenpeace.org/comms/cbio/
brazil.html and use some of the information
in your rain forest report.

DEFORESTATION

People cutting down trees is slowly leading to areas of deforestation around the world. In South America, an area of rain forest the size of a football field is cut down every second. People use the wood as building material for furniture and fuel for heating and cooking. Sometimes areas of land are cleared for farmland or for new settlements. The loss of these trees also means the loss of many animals and plants in these areas.

SUSTAINABLE FORESTRY

Many people are working to encourage sustainable forestry around the world. With sustainable forestry, people will replant forests and leave some untouched. Wood that has been grown in this way is marked with a logo, such as the Forest Stewardship Council (FSC) logo. Encourage your family to buy only wood

and wooden furniture that carries these marks. In Acre, Brazil, the government has a plan to use the forests in a sustainable way. If farmers cut down trees to plant their crops, they must plant a variety of new trees to replace the trees they cut down. Some grow quickly, such as banana trees, and others, such as apple and mahogany trees, take longer. Also, the Brazilian government allows logging only in certain areas. Because the government makes sure that the logging companies plant new trees to replace those that were removed, there will still be forests in the future.

RAIN FOREST WRITING

Prepare an essay about Brazil and its tropical rain forests. Discuss the various plans people have to use and preserve the rain forests; find out what types of trees are in high demand and which plants and animals are in danger.

How to use energy

Think about your day so far. Have you turned on any lights, listened to the radio, or walked to school? All of these activities required energy. Eating food gave you the energy to learn and play at school, just as burning fossil fuels in power stations provides the electricity needed to power the radio and light your home.

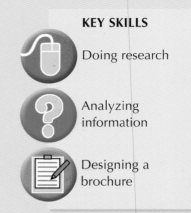

KEY SKILLS

Doing research

Analyzing information

Designing a brochure

City lights in Tokyo, Japan. In the future, people will have to find other sources of power because fossil fuels are running out.

NONRENEWABLE ENERGY

Most of the energy we use today to power cars, keep houses warm, cook food, and make machines work comes from nonrenewable energy sources such as fossil fuels. Coal, oil, and gas are all fossil fuels that formed millions of years ago from the fossilized remains of plants and animals. People are using fossil fuels quickly, and eventually they will run out. Fossil fuels also produce pollution when they are burned. Pollution affects the air we breathe and the balance of gases in the earth's protective atmosphere.

RENEWABLE ENERGY

Some people think that renewable energy is the answer to our future energy needs. Renewable energy will never run out because it uses energy from the sun (solar power), wind (wind power), water (hydroelectricity), and plants (biofuel) to make electricity. Solar panels absorb heat energy from the sun and use it to heat water and generate electricity. Wind power is generated by huge wind turbines located in open spaces. Hydroelectricity is produced by damming a river and then using the trapped water to turn a huge wheel, which generates electricity. Biofuel, also called digester gas, is the gas produced by the fermentation of organic matter, including manure, wastewater sludge, municipal solid waste, or any other biodegradable material.

A hydroelectric dam on the Rhine River in Germany.

While renewable energy does not cause pollution, it can create other problems. For example, areas of land are flooded to form reservoirs for hydroelectricity projects. These reservoirs store the water before it flows through electricity generators. However, through this process, some people lose their homes and land forever.

Use the Internet to find out about a dam project that generates renewable energy—for example, the Lesotho Highlands Water project. Use the Web site at www.lhwp.org.ls as a starting point to find out where the project is, what it does, how it affects the local community, and how it is working toward a sustainable future. Then, use a computer to design a brochure to inform other people about the project.

Climate change

Our climate is the average weather we experience over a long period of time. Scientists can show us that there have always been changes in climate throughout the earth's long history, and weather records show that some decades have been hotter than others. However, in the past several decades, the climate has been changing at a much faster rate, and there are much more extreme weather patterns around the world.

KEY SKILLS

Looking at global issues

Interpreting maps

Doing research

Designing a poster

GLOBAL WARMING

Many scientists think that the world climate is changing because human activity is upsetting the balance of carbon dioxide in the earth's atmosphere. The atmosphere forms a protective blanket around the earth, shielding it from the sun's harmful rays while allowing the sun's heat to reach the earth. Levels of some gases in the atmosphere, such as carbon dioxide (CO_2), prevent excess heat energy from escaping back into space. Gradually, this natural process, called the greenhouse effect, is causing global temperatures to rise more quickly because of pollution in the atmosphere. Changes in the earth's temperature combined with rising sea levels will have a devastating impact on low-lying countries and many coastal areas and marine habitats.

This illustration shows how the temperature of the earth's surface is rising. Many scientists believe that emissions from factories and traffic are speeding up the process.

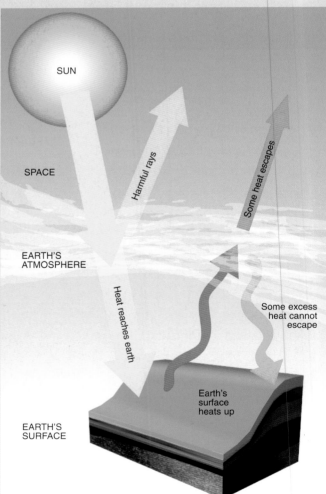

SUN

SPACE

Harmful rays

Some heat escapes

EARTH'S ATMOSPHERE

Heat reaches earth

Some excess heat cannot escape

Earth's surface heats up

EARTH'S SURFACE

WHAT CAN BE DONE?

On an international level, world leaders have met on several occasions to discuss plans to reduce the speed of climate change. In 1995 in Kyoto, Japan, some governments agreed that only more economically developed countries (MEDCs) should have to cut CO_2 emissions. LEDCs were not required to reduce their CO_2 emissions because they were low at that time.

This illustration shows the different levels of carbon dioxide (CO_2) produced by each country. The green countries have the highest emissions.

Since 1995, the economies of some LEDCs, such as India and China, have grown rapidly, and as a result, their CO_2 emissions have risen. Today, the international community feels that these countries should reduce their emissions. In addition, the U.S. refused to sign the Kyoto agreement despite the fact that it produces high levels of CO_2. So there is still a high amount of CO_2 gas being pumped into our atmosphere.

Look at the map below to see which countries produce the highest levels of CO_2. Are there more emissions in LEDCs or MEDCs? Why do you think this happens?

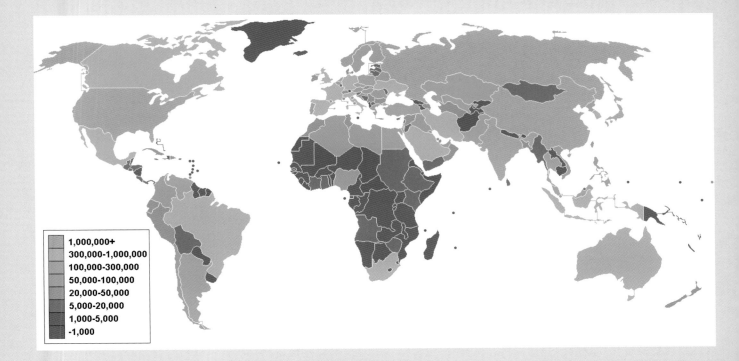

1,000,000+
300,000-1,000,000
100,000-300,000
50,000-100,000
20,000-50,000
5,000-20,000
1,000-5,000
-1,000

PERSONAL ENERGY PLAN

We can all help reduce climate change by taking action in our everyday lives. Just remembering to turn off lights, asking parents to use energy-saving lightbulbs, wearing more clothes rather than turning up the heat, and turning off computers and televisions instead of leaving them on standby will save a lot of energy in a year. It will also reduce electricity bills! Go to www.ase.org. for many more ideas on how to save energy. Look at their "6° of Energy Efficiency Challenge," then use some of your new knowledge to produce your own energy-saving plan. Design a poster to encourage others to use less energy to slow down climate change. Ask to display the poster in your school.

Earthquakes

Earthquakes are one of the most destructive natural hazards on the earth. They occur at the point where one of the earth's plates (that form the earth's outer layer) becomes stuck when it slides against another plate. Pressure builds under the earth's surface until the plate jolts free, causing the ground to move violently—an earthquake. Depending on how many people are living in the area, the earthquake's strength, and the area's economic development, earthquakes can cause loss of life and damage to buildings.

KEY SKILLS

Doing research

Writing a report; making comparisons

Looking at photographs

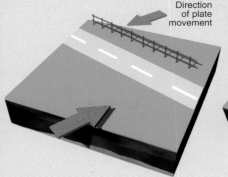

This road and fence are built across a fault line. Two of the earth's plates are sliding past each other.

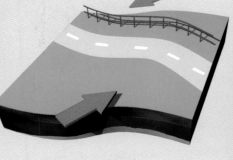

Over time, the plates move but they are stuck along the fault line. Pressure builds up underground.

Suddenly, energy is released from underground as the plates jolt free. This point underground, shown as a red dot, is called the focus. The movement releases shockwaves— called seismic waves—in all directions. The epicenter, shown as a yellow dot, is directly above the focus at the surface. This is usually where the most damage occurs.

THE SAN FRANCISCO STORY

In 1906, an earthquake in San Francisco, California, almost completely destroyed the city. About 3,000 people were killed, and more than half of the city's population (about 225,000 people) were made homeless. It took days to control the fires that broke out all over the city. Yet a strong earthquake in the same city in 1989 caused only 63 deaths, with 3,500 injuries and damage to 100,000 buildings.

RESEARCH AND REPORT

Go to the Internet site of The Virtual Museum of the City of San Francisco at www.sfmuseum.org to read reports of both the 1906 and 1989 earthquakes and see photographs of the damage. Use some of this information to write a report comparing the two earthquakes, highlighting how the city's planning reduced deaths.

CAN PEOPLE BE PROTECTED FROM EARTHQUAKES?

There are some measures that people can take to prepare for earthquakes, but nothing can protect people completely. In MEDCs, such as Japan and the United States, all new buildings and road structures in earthquake zones are built to strict anti-earthquake standards. These buildings absorb some of the power of the earthquakes. People living in earthquake zones are encouraged to keep an earthquake pack at home, including a first-aid kit, canned food, and a battery-powered radio. In Japan, people receive earthquake emergency training to reduce panic and deaths. In MEDCs, money is spent on up-to-date monitoring of earthquake zones in order to help predict earthquakes.

The aftermath of the earthquake that rocked San Francisco in 1989. Safety plans helped save many lives.

HELPING HAND

Earthquake strength is measured by a machine called a seismometer. It produces a graph that shows the strength of the earth's movements. The strength is measured using the Richter Scale, where higher numbers represent the strongest earthquakes.

In LEDCs, buildings are often constructed to lower standards, so they are more likely to collapse during an earthquake. Emergency services are often less equipped for a quick response, so it can be days or even weeks before help or emergency supplies reach remote areas. With less money available, it takes longer to rebuild damaged buildings and repair roads and railways.

2005 PAKISTAN EARTHQUAKE

Research the 2005 Pakistan earthquake and compare it with the information you gathered on the San Francisco earthquake of 1989 in the activity above. Start by logging on to news.bbc.co.uk/1/hi/in_depth/south_asia/2005/south_asia_quake/default.stm and reading the archived news report.

Reduce, reuse, recycle

Many items that we throw away every day could be reused or recycled. Recycling means putting a material, such as glass, paper, or metal, through a process so that it can be used again. Reusing products means finding a second use for them or finding a new owner.

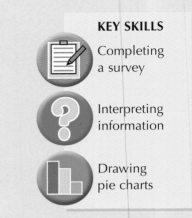

RECYCLE

Recycling products reduces the demand for raw materials and reduces the amount of waste. New York City produces 37,000 tons (34,000 t) of garbage every day, of which 50 percent is paper that could be recycled. All of this waste has to be disposed of to keep the city clean. Some waste is burned in incinerators; other waste is buried in landfill sites. Once materials, such as paper or glass, have been disposed of,

they are usually lost forever. By recycling things made of paper and glass, the raw materials inside them are kept in use.

Every ton of recycled paper prevents approximately 17 trees from being cut down and saves 4,100 kilowatts of electricity—enough to heat the average home for six months.

This paper was collected from homes as part of a local recycling program.

PERSONAL ACTION PLAN

There are many ways that we can all reduce, reuse, or recycle materials to save resources or relieve pressure on landfill sites. Here are a few ideas:

- Keep paper, cardboard, glass, plastics, textiles, and metals separate from other household garbage. Find out if these items can be collected from your home or persuade your parents or guardians to take them to recycling collection points.
- If you have a yard, ask your parents or guardians to get a compost bin and use it to collect vegetable peelings and garden waste. Eventually, this will form compost to improve the soil in your yard.
- If you live in a house, ask an adult to attach a rain barrel to the drainpipe and collect rain water. Reuse this on your yard or garden rather than using new water.
- Buy food and other products that have minimum packaging. You will not have to throw as much away.
- Take bags to the supermarket instead of using new bags each time.
- When shopping, buy recycled paper products if possible, including envelopes and paper.
- Take unwanted games, household items, books, and clothes to thrift stores. These can then be reused by somebody else.
- Cell phones, printer cartridges, even bicycles, can all be recycled or repaired by people. Log on to www.epa.gov/ecycling to find out how to do this in the U.S.

RECYCLING SURVEY

Make a table like the one shown below. List 10 household waste products (we started the list for you) and then survey ten people to find out what they normally do with these particular products. Do they throw them away, reuse them, or recycle them?

Present your data as a pie chart showing the proportion of products recycled or reused and those that are thrown away. Your pie chart may look something like this:

WASTE PRODUCT	GARBAGE	RECYCLE/REUSE
Apple core and skin		
Empty juice carton		
Old cell phone		
Old T-shirt		
Empty glass bottle		

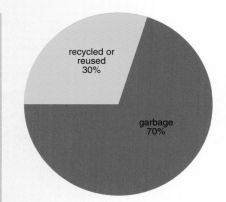

recycled or reused 30%

garbage 70%

25

Overpopulation

Each country has its own resources, such as soil, water, land, and minerals, that support the people living there. In countries where the population is high or quickly rising, people are more likely to have a low standard of living or be threatened by famine because there are not enough resources for everyone. Governments create plans to solve the problem of overpopulation in their country.

FOCUS ON CHINA

During the 20th century, the population of China was growing at an alarming rate. The government of China worried about how they would feed all of these people and announced a "one child policy" in 1979 to slow down the birthrate. This meant that married couples could have only one child by law. The child would receive benefits, such as free education and healthcare, as well as priority housing. A second child would receive no education or healthcare. Look at the two population pyramids for China in 1990 and 2006. Predict how the pyramid will look in 2050. What impact has the policy had on Chinese population growth?

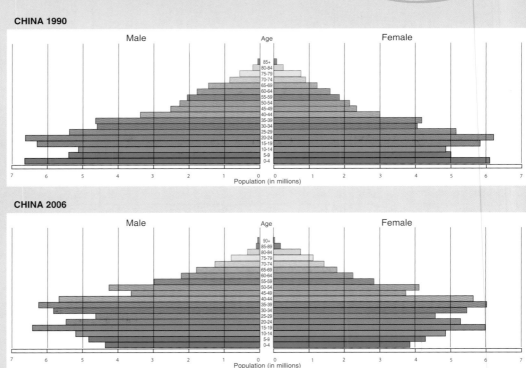

CHINA 1990

CHINA 2006

FOCUS ON SOUTHERN INDIA

In Kerala, a state in southern India, the local government decided that education, rather than forced policies, was the best way to reduce birthrates. Here, women and girls had to attend school by law, enabling many of them to get better jobs after leaving school. The girls went to sex education classes to help them plan their families.

Since the start of this program, 2,800 villages have formed "mandals," or community organizations. These mandals run childcare centers, adult literacy classes, welfare services, and activities to improve the status of women. All of these encourage women to have fewer babies, and today, Kerala is no longer an overpopulated state.

Of the two policies discussed, which do you think is the better way to curb overpopulation? Which policy is more sustainable?

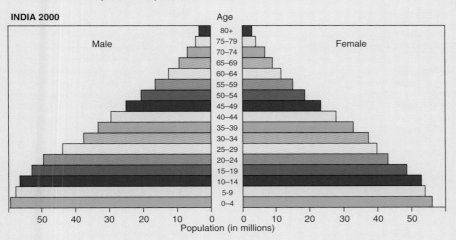

INDIA 2000

Age

Male

Female

80+
75–79
70–74
65–69
60–64
55–59
50–54
45–49
40–44
35–39
30–34
25–29
20–24
15–19
10–14
5-9
0–4

50   40   30   20   10   0   0   10   20   30   40   50

Population (in millions)

Women and children in rural India are given sex education lessons. Many people believe education will help control birthrates in the future.

Underpopulation

Underpopulation occurs in countries where the birthrate is falling. As a result, the population of the country gets smaller and there is a higher percentage of older people. Some countries, such as Italy, Japan, and Russia, are worried that they will not have enough people in the future to do all the jobs that are necessary for the country to function.

KEY SKILLS

Looking at global issues

Using the Internet

Interpreting information

Looking at population pyramids

The population of many MEDCs will change over the next 30 years. People who live in Japan are waiting longer to have children or not having any at all.

WHY ARE BIRTHRATES DIFFERENT?

The cost of living in some countries, such as Japan, is extremely high. By the time a young couple has paid for housing, food, water, and electricity, they may feel that they can afford to only have one child or none at all. Some women, in particular, may decide not to have children because they are enjoying their career and the lifestyle it brings them. In addition, advances in medicine and a better standard of living mean that many people are living longer lives than in the past, which leads to an aging population.

HELPING HAND
Population pyramids also show information about life expectancy. Pyramids in many countries are becoming square as people live longer.

PLANNING FOR FUTURE GENERATIONS

In the way that some countries have formed plans to reduce their populations, others are looking for ways to increase their population. For example, the authorities in the UK, New Zealand, and Australia encourage economic migrants to fill the job gaps caused by the countries' falling birthrates. If the country does not have enough teachers or doctors, then teachers and doctors from other countries are given work permits and encouraged to move or migrate. Not everybody agrees with this policy because it leaves the country of origin with fewer doctors and teachers. This process is called "brain drain." In Russia, the government has tried something completely different. They have actively encouraged women to have more babies and offer prizes and rewards for those who do.

COMPARING POPULATION PYRAMIDS

Log on to the following Web site http://www.census.gov/ipc/www/idbpyr.html to find population pyramids for your country and compare it to the pyramid below.

What challenges will Japan face in the next 30 years? How do these challenges compare with those that your country will face? Should people work longer so that the population is more sustainable? How do these pyramids compare with those for China and India shown on pages 26–27?

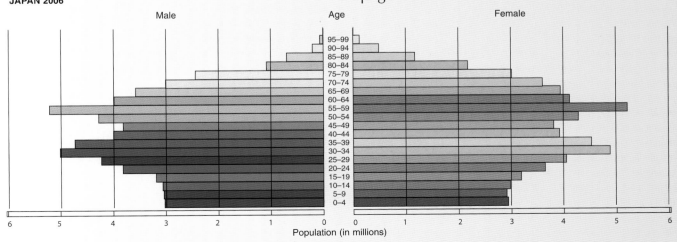

JAPAN 2006

Settlements in the future

The places where people live are called settlements. Settlements are organized into a hierarchy with small hamlets and villages near the bottom and large cities at the top. As countries develop, people migrate to the bigger settlements for work and the chance to improve their standard of living. However, some cities have grown too quickly, leaving poorer people with low-quality housing and limited services.

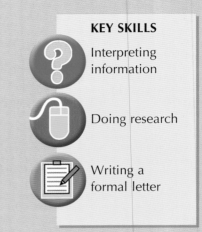

Settlements can be organized in order of their importance to form a settlement hierarchy. There are fewer cities, so they are at the top of the pyramid.

CITY

TOWN

VILLAGE

HAMLET

MEGACITIES

There are more than 280 cities in the world that have more than one million residents, and these very large cities are causing concern for planners as they continue to grow and sprawl out into the surrounding countryside. Some cities, such as Mexico City, Los Angeles, and Tokyo, have more than 10 million inhabitants and are sometimes called megacities. Other huge cities, such as those on the eastern coast of the U.S., have spread into each other and formed a huge megalopolis stretching from Boston to Washington, DC. This huge urban area has become known as "Boswash."

URBAN PROBLEMS

When places grow rapidly, problems often emerge. In Mexico City, housing development cannot keep up with the rise in population, so people are forced to build homes out of any materials they can find. These slum dwellings build up in areas called favelas or shantytowns, where the standard of living is very poor. Mexico City also has high levels of traffic congestion, leading to poor air quality and transportation around the city. In addition, 12,125 tons (11,000 t) of garbage are created every day, but there are only resources to collect 9,920 tons (9,000 t) so a lot of the garbage is left in the streets.

SUSTAINABLE DEVELOPMENT

Some countries are looking at ways to allow cities to grow without ruining the area for current residents or future generations. For example, in the UK, town and city planners have created "green belts" around many towns and cities to restrain their growth and preserve green spaces, such as forests and parks. Development in these green spaces is severely restricted.

SUSTAINABLE CITY

Curitiba, Brazil, is considered to be one of the most sustainable cities in the world. Many people who live there are happy with their city. The mayor, Jaimie Lerner, was largely responsible for the success of the settlement. He and the other people in power enjoyed solving problems by listening to the people of the city and keeping solutions small scale and practical. Their garbage problem was solved by giving poor people money for every bag of garbage they brought to the recycling center. The traffic congestion problem was solved by banning cars from most areas and replanting these areas with flowers and grass. The traffic was rerouted into one-way streets with some streets reserved for buses. The buses run past the apartment complexes, encouraging residents to use public transportation rather than their cars. Favelas still exist, but the city often employs single mothers from these areas, and architects help build homes affordably, one room at a time.

ACTION PLAN

Using Curitiba as a model, can you think of ways that the public officials of Mexico City could improve the standard of living for its current and future residents? Prepare a letter to the public officials of Mexico City, detailing your findings. Remember to use formal language in your letter.

Mexico City, like many large cities, has grown rapidly and is now facing problems associated with overcrowding and pollution.

HELPING HAND
Find out more about cities at www.un.org/cyberschoolbus/habitat/index.asp—part of the UN cities program.

Fair trade

If every country in the world had to exist on its own, there would not be many different things for its population to buy or eat, and the country would not be very wealthy. To solve this problem, countries trade with one another. They sell, or export, the things that they grow or make and buy, or import, the things that they cannot grow or make.

UNFAIR TRADING

While trading can result in economic growth and employment for people, many trading arrangements are not fair to the producers of goods. For example, because consumers in MEDCs want cheap clothes and clothing companies want big profits, many of the clothes in our shops are made in "sweatshops" in LEDCs. In sweatshops, people work long hours for very little wages. Many food products are also grown where the lowest possible wage is paid to the farmer or farmworker. With few other job opportunities, many families are forced to struggle in poverty and often cannot afford to educate their children.

A worker dumps cocoa beans on a fair trade farm in Ghana.

FAIR TRADING

One solution to this problem is to encourage fair trading. Fair trade is about paying a fair price to the producer for their product, whether it is bananas, cocoa beans, or cotton. In addition, the buyer pays a "social premium"—an extra sum of money—which is used in the producers' community to improve healthcare, education, or services. Long-term business relationships are set up between producers and buyers so that farmers know they will have a market for their goods at a fair and fixed price. There are many examples of fair trade success stories. For example, the Divine brand of chocolate candy sold in the U.S. is made from cocoa grown by farmers in the Kuapa Kokoo cooperative in Ghana, West Africa.

HELPING HAND
To find out more about Divine fair trade chocolate, visit www.divinechocolateusa.com/

SUPPORTING FAIR TRADE

You may have noticed the "Fair Trade Certified" logo on the packaging of some of the foods you eat or that are available in stores. Visit http://transfairusa.org to see the logo and find out more about fair trade products. You can help improve the lifestyles of farmers in LEDCs by choosing foods with this label and persuading others to buy them, too. Sometimes the fair trade food may be more expensive than foods that are not fair trade products, but a much greater portion of the price of the food has benefited the farmer who grew the food. Many different foods carry the logo, such as coffee, chocolate, sugar, fruit, and rice.

Complete a survey of how many fair trade products a group of ten people buy. You may want to set up a table like the one below, adding other products.

FAIRLY TRADED PRODUCT	NUMBER OF PEOPLE WHO BUY IT
rice	
coffee	
sugar	
fruit	
chocolate	

Using the data you have collected, make a bar graph similar to the one below:

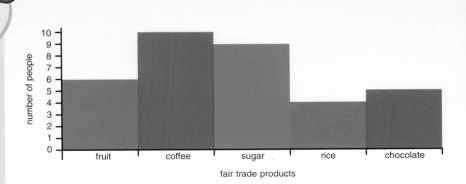

City transportation

As places develop and people become wealthier, higher demands are placed on transportation. Many roads become congested and air quality deteriorates. Many of the major cities of the world, such as Mexico City, London, Tokyo, Paris, and Shanghai, share this problem.

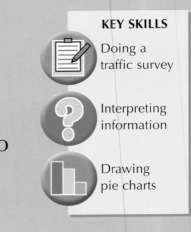

KEY SKILLS

Doing a traffic survey

Interpreting information

Drawing pie charts

GOING UNDERGROUND

One solution is to build more road and train systems underground. Developers believe these will reduce congestion and improve air quality above ground. The city of Boston, Massachusetts, has recently started a massive underground road project, named the "Big Dig," to relieve some of the traffic congestion. Many people believe that more roads only encourage more traffic, and that road building is not a sustainable solution. Many cities, including Paris and New York, have underground train systems that efficiently move many people around. These are expensive, but they provide a good option for city travel in the future.

Part of the underground network, called the Big Dig, in Boston, Massachusetts. Developers hope to move some traffic from the overground roads.

RIDING THE BUS

A bus occupies the space of three cars but can carry 40 or more people. If more people used buses, it would reduce the number of cars on the roads. However, when people have experienced slow commutes by bus due to traffic jams, they often prefer to control their journey by traveling by car. To solve this problem, many urban areas have introduced dedicated bus lanes. The buses use these to bypass traffic jams and provide a better alternative to individual car travel.

Bus lanes might encourage people to use buses, but bus travel still has to be affordable. In Bremen, Germany, the price of a bus ticket has been subsidized by the government, making it cheaper to buy. At the same time, in some places such as London, traffic into the downtown area has been reduced by introducing a congestion charge—a fee that must be paid for going downtown.

The monorail in Sydney, Australia is one of many transportation programs built in cities around the world to reduce traffic congestion.

CONDUCT A TRAFFIC SURVEY

With a friend, plan and conduct a traffic survey in your local area to compare how many people use public transportation and how many use private cars. Choose the location of the survey—maybe at a traffic light or an intersection—making sure that you stand in a safe area and can see the traffic clearly. One person counts the number of cars and buses that drive past you, while the other records how many people are in each vehicle (you might have to estimate the number of people on a bus). Write the results on a table like the one below.

Which type of transportation was more popular? Use the data from your survey to draw pie charts. The first pie chart should compare the number of vehicles and the second should compare the number of people traveling. What do your results tell you about the two types of transportation?

	number of vehicles	number of people
cars		
buses		

DEVELOPING OTHER FORMS OF TRANSPORTATION

The city authority of Sydney, Australia, has developed a monorail that transports people above the existing roads. In Manchester, UK, and San Francisco, California, tram networks have been developed to carry people along a set route.

Controlling tourism

Tourism is the fastest growing industry and creates many jobs. It employs about 10 percent of all people of working age worldwide, although many of these jobs are low paying, part-time positions. Sometimes too many tourists can cause problems for the places they visit, and traveling vast distances by airplane or car causes pollution. Sustainable plans must be made to ensure the earth survives for future generations.

KEY SKILLS

Designing a hotel; drawing a sketch map

Doing research

Interpreting information

Tourists fill a beach on Mallorca, an island in the Mediterranean Sea. Increasing numbers of people are able to afford vacations abroad.

FAIR TOURISM

Fair tourism is about looking after the staff and using as many local resources and services as possible in the tourist industry. The Backpack Hostel in Cape Town, South Africa, is a perfect example of this. The profits from the hostel are shared with the community. For example, a crèche, or day care, has been built for small children to attend while their parents work. As much food as possible is bought from local farmers, and local people are employed and involved in the running of the hostel. Local artists display and sell their work in the hostel, too. The result is that local people benefit from tourism and are treated fairly.

This hut is part of an ecotourism project in South Africa.

ECOTOURISM

Ecotourism works to generate money and create jobs for local people, while protecting the local environment and culture in a sustainable way. In 2003, the community of Piedra Blanca, Ecuador decided to try to improve its economic situation by developing an ecotourism project. Visitors stay in the village, paying villagers for accommodation. Local guides have been fully trained and take turns accompanying the tourists. This allows all of the guides to earn money from the tourists. There are strict rules to protect the people's culture as well. For example, tourists must wear suitable clothing and obey the rules of the forest. The money that the villagers make allows them to work on local conservation and reforestation plans.

WHAT CAN YOU DO?

Flying is a quick way to reach your vacation destination. However, airplanes are huge polluters and flying increases your "eco footprint" (see page 9). When you go on vacation, remember to eat local food whenever possible and watch for fair tourism or ecotourism trips.

DESIGN A HOTEL

Use the Internet and the information you have learned to design an ecofriendly hotel. Before you start designing the building, think about the following:

- What materials will be used to build the hotel?
- What type of power will you use in the hotel?
- Who will run the hotel?
- How will the profits be used?
- Where will the food come from?

Once you have decided these factors, sketch a map of the hotel and show the sustainable features.

Our food

Forty years ago, the ordinary diet for most people consisted of food that was grown and sold locally. Today, some foods are transported thousands of miles to stores using air transportation or shipping; this causes environmental problems. Also, in some cases, food resources are being exploited in a way that is not sustainable. For example, overfishing in one area causes fish populations to get so low that there may not be enough fish for people in the future.

KEY SKILLS

Keeping a food diary

Looking at food labels

Cargo is unloaded from a plane. Food is transported to our stores from all around the world.

TIGERS

BOEING 747-200F   N807FT

Demands on fish populations mean that quotas may get even smaller in future.

FOOD TRANSPORTATION

Transporting food contributes to climate change because fossil fuels power planes and trucks. People are now calculating the distance food is transported to reach stores. For example, an apple grown in New Zealand travels approximately 22,800 miles (36,700 km) to reach stores in the U.S., while a locally grown variety may only have traveled a few miles. Eating food that is in season locally can reduce this figure.

FISHING QUOTAS AND MARINE RESERVES

To prevent overfishing, quotas can be set to limit the amount of fish that can be caught in a particular area each year. An alternative is to establish marine reserves. This has been done successfully around Australia, where young fish can now grow to full size in the protected marine reserves and then be released. Then, there is always a new population of fish growing for the next generation.

SUSTAINABLE FARMING

After World War II (1939–45), farmers in the UK were encouraged to produce more food, and this led to intensive farming practices. Wetlands were drained, hedges removed, and the use of chemical fertilizers and pesticides became widespread. All of this has harmed the environment. Greater priority is now being given to encouraging farmers to use sustainable methods. These include using less fertilizer, or using natural fertilizers, and introducing certain insects to keep pests under control. Some farmers now farm organically or without pesticides.

THINK GLOBAL, ACT LOCAL

Keep a food diary for one week, recording everything you eat and where it came from, if possible. At the end of the week, look at what you have eaten and try to come up with seasonal or more local alternatives to the food that has traveled the farthest.

Breaking out of poverty

If the world were a village of 100 people, the richest person would have more wealth than the poorest 57 people combined. The poorest people are said to be "in poverty." There are two types of poverty—relative and absolute. Relative poverty is when people cannot afford to buy luxuries such as computers. Although life might be a struggle, conditions are not life-threatening. Absolute poverty is when life itself is threatened. In absolute poverty, a person may not receive an education, be able to afford decent housing or enough food, or have access to clean drinking water.

This family in Mexico lives in absolute poverty. They have no running water, no electricity, and they cannot afford good-quality housing.

KEY SKILLS

Doing research

Understanding global issues

CISIRA, SOUTH AFRICA

Consider Cisira, a small village in eastern Cape Province, South Africa. There is no running water and the 400 people who live there have to drink dirty water from the river. One way to avoid drinking the dirty water is to buy bottled water from a local supplier, but most people cannot afford to buy bottled water. As a result, they get sick from drinking the dirty water, but they cannot afford to go to the doctor for medicine. When people become ill, they cannot go to work, so they do not earn any money. This means that they cannot buy food, and it is more difficult to recover. Sick children cannot go to school, so they do not get an education, and as a result, they will not be able to get a job that pays well. This is known as the cycle of poverty, and it is very difficult to break.

HELPING THE PEOPLE OF CISIRA

There is a sustainable solution. Water for the People is a program that has improved access to clean water for two million people in Africa. Thanks to Ondeo Services, Cisira now has pipes connecting the village to a clean water supply. The residents can buy water with special "smart cards." The water costs up to 40 percent less than bottled water. To get the pipes in place, trenches had to be dug and pipes were installed. Most of these jobs went to local people, so they earned money to spend on their children's education and to buy more food. They now have a chance to escape the cycle of poverty.

SEND-A-GOAT!

In Kenya, 55,000 people have escaped poverty as a result of a project called Farm Friends, run by Farm Africa. To find out how this program works, go to Farm Africa's Web site: www.farmafrica.org.uk and click on their Farm Friends section. When you have learned all about it, ask your parents, guardians, or teachers if they would like to become involved. Perhaps you and your friends could collect the money to buy a farm animal for a family in Africa. Your school could run a charity fund-raising event to buy goats or other farm animals through the Farm Friends program.

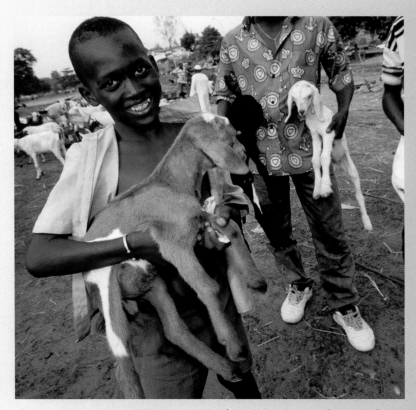

Goats are very important in many African countries. They produce milk and can be sold for money or slaughtered for their meat.

Reducing the Digital Divide

If the world were a village of a 100 people, 80 of them would never have heard a telephone dial tone or used a computer. The difference between those that have telecommunications technology and those that do not is called the Digital Divide. It is generally thought that those groups of people without access to technology will fall farther and farther behind those that do, suffering a much poorer standard of living. Some attempts are being made to solve this problem for the future.

KEY SKILLS

Looking at global issues

Doing research

Completing a report

HEALTHNET

In many places, health workers are unable to stay in contact with other people or up-to-date with the latest information on how to treat illnesses. HealthNet is helping reduce the Digital Divide by putting those people working in remote areas in contact with other health workers. There is no need for telephone lines because satellite communications are used to reach the most inaccessible areas.

A health worker in rural Gambia can take a picture with a digital camera to record a patient's symptoms. These pictures are then sent to a nearby town where a doctor can diagnose the illness. The patient can then be properly treated.

This doctor is talking to a health worker via satellite link. New technology is helping reduce the Digital Divide.

GRAMEENPHONE

In Bangladesh, a cell phone company is pioneering the "Village Phone" program. By giving small loans to people to buy cell phones, the program helps the poorest people earn a living. Jamirum lives in a small village an hour from the capital, Dhaka. She bought a phone through this project. Her phone is the only one in an area where 3,500 people live. Jamirum charges people a small amount to use her phone and makes a profit of about $140.00 a month—nearly four times the average wage in Bangladesh. Using the phone means that people can stay in touch with relatives who live in other towns or countries. Farmers can get the local weather report and check prices for their crops. The phones can also be used to give people advanced notice of cyclones. With this information, they can reach safety in time.

This woman in Ghana, Africa, is using a cell phone to talk to her relatives. A phone like this one can connect people in rural areas.

RESEARCH AND REPORT

Use the Internet to research the Digital Divide in India—a country with a booming telecommunications industry in some places, such as Bangalore, while in other areas, many villagers have never used computers or cell phones. Start by looking at www.newsbbc.co.uk and then search for "Digital Divide India." Use the information to write a report comparing the different experiences of telecommunications in India.

Glossary

Absolute poverty
When people lack the basic things needed to survive such as food, shelter, and clean drinking water.

Atmosphere
The mixture of gases that surrounds the earth.

Biodegradable
Describing a substance that breaks down, or decomposes, naturally.

Birthrate
The number of people born each year for every 1,000 people in an area or group.

Carbon dioxide (CO₂)
An invisible gas found naturally in air. It is released when fossil fuels are burned and is one of the biggest contributers to global warming.

Climate
The average weather conditions of a certain area.

Climate change
A general change in climate that may be due to natural causes or the effects of human activity in the form of pollution and global warming.

Death rate
Also called the mortality rate. The number of people who die each year for every 1,000 people in an area or group.

Deforestation
The destruction of forests for building, farming, or other use of the wood.

Drainage basin
The area of land that is drained by a river system.

Eco footprint
The estimated area of land and sea affected by a single person's lifestyle, measured in global acres.

Epicenter
The point on the earth's surface directly above the focus of an earthquake.

Erosion
The loosening of weathered material by the wind, water, or ice.

Fair trade
Trading to ensure that a product's producers, such as cocoa farmers or cotton pickers, benefit from its sale.

Floodplain
The wide, flat valley floor characteristic of the lower course of a river, which is often flooded by river water.

Global warming
A gradual increase in the average temperature of the earth's atmosphere.

Green belt
A strip of protected park or farmland at the edge of a city, designed to prevent urban sprawl.

Greenhouse gases
Gases that trap heat in the earth's atmosphere.

Groins
Fence-like structures on a beach that trap material and increase beach depth.

Habitat
The environment where a plant or an animal usually grows or lives.

Hard engineering
Structures to control geographical processes such as flooding or coastal erosion.

Holistic planning
Considering the sustainable care of something, such as a river, in terms of the whole thing rather than its individual parts.

Intensive farming
Farming to produce maximum crop or animal yields from a limited area of land.

Less economically developed country (LEDC)
A country in which the majority of the population lives in poverty. These countries tend to be mainly rural, but often, their cities are growing fast.

Life expectancy
The expected life span of a person, measured in years and often taken as an average across a population.

Logging
The removal of trees from a forest to be sold as lumber.

More economically developed country (MEDC)
A country with much greater wealth per person and more developed industry than a less economically developed country.

Quota
A limited amount imposed on something; for example, the number of fish allowed to be caught in an area of water.

Rural
In the countryside.

Soft engineering
Using natural environmental processes to cope with geographical problems such as flooding or coastal erosion.

Sustainability
The ability to meet the needs of people and environments today and to maintain them in the future.

Urban
In towns and cities.

Web sites

www.earthsummit.info
This Web site contains many other links for you to find out more about sustainable development.

www.unesco.org/water
The "water page" of the United Nations Educational, Scientific, and Cultural Organization.

www.nilebasin.org/nilemap.htm
Web site of the Nile Basin Initiative showing a map of the Nile River. It also has links to other sites about the Nile River.

www.worldlandtrust.org
Web site of this wildlife action group that is campaigning to save habitats, including forests, throughout the world.

www.foei.org
Home page of Friends of the Earth International, featuring up-to-date news about their environmental campaigns.

www.greenpeace.org/international
The Greenpeace International Web site that includes climate change and deforestation campaign news.

www.iiees.ac.ir/english/index_e.asp
Web site of the International Institute of Earthquake Engineering and Seismology.

www.overpopulation.org
Web site of World Population Awareness, featuring a lot of information about why population matters to our future.

Note to parents and teachers:

Every effort has been made to ensure that these Web sites are suitable for children, that they are of the highest educational value, and that they contain no inappropriate or offensive material. However, because of the nature of the Internet, it is impossible to guarantee that the contents of these sites will not be altered. We strongly advise that Internet access be supervised by a responsible adult.

Index